SISTER RAVEN, BROTHER HARE

A Journal for Those Who Honor Animal Magic

by Mary Sojourner
Illustrations by Lawrence Ormsby

NORTHLAND PUBLISHING

Copyright © 1992 by Northland Publishing
All rights reserved.

This book may not be reproduced in whole or in part, by any means (with the exception of short quotes for the purpose of review), without permission of the publisher. For information, address Northland Publishing Co., P.O. Box 1389, Flagstaff, Arizona 86002.

FIRST EDITION

ISBN 0-87358-537-2
Library of Congress Catalog Card Number 91-44907
Composed and Printed in the United States of America

Designed by Carolyn Gibbs
Cover Design by David Jenney

Cataloging-in-Publication Data
Sojourner, Mary.
    Sister Raven, Brother Hare : a journal for those who honor animal magic : quotes / by and complied by Mary Sojourner. -- 1st ed.
    176 p.
    Includes bibliographical references (p.176).
    ISBN 0-87358-537-2 (softcover) : $9.95
    1. Diaries (Blank-books) 2. Animals--Quotations, maxims, etc. I. Title.
CT9999.S64   1992   91-44907
818'.5402--dc20   CIP

4-92/5M/0380

Sister Raven, Brother Hare is bare sand for your tracks. It is a map. You might follow it or break your own trail. I have included quotes—some from my own writing and experiences, some from various delightful sources, which are listed in the back. Find them. Read them. Let the pictures fill your heart.

These Thoughts Belong To:

For Bill,
who knows enough to know
he doesn't know...

And for those who do not write or speak in human talk, for those who purr and howl and squeak and crrkkk and scream and sing, for those who stalk and slither and crawl and swim and fly, for those who hunt and those who are hunted...that we may know we are blessed to share this earth with these brothers and sisters... and that we may speak out for them against those who, for profit, greed, and power, would see them gone.

So be it...

Introduction

I AM CAMPED AT THE BASE OF A RAPID on the San Juan River in southern Utah. I am fifty and have just rowed white water for the first time. My friend and I sleep apart, in harmony, about one hundred feet above the rapid. As I float into sleep, the water roars and whispers in my ears. The last thing I see is Orion, glittering above the black canyon wall. He prowls in the East, upriver from a single, bent juniper.

I look up and see Orion moving, Lepur at his feet, star man hunting through the stars for the shining hare he will never catch. I wonder if I'm dreaming, close my eyes, breathe two times, it seems, maybe three, look up again and see the shining hunter farther East. I believe I'm awake, close my eyes, and hear, in a minute's time, the history of humans in Utah: bare feet running on sandstone, horses' hooves on river rock, wagon wheels, dynamite blasts, mine shafts tearing into the earth, whistles, trains, a city going up, sawblades through wood, hammers on nails, the buildings rising with a shout. I open my eyes. There are only canyon walls and obsidian sky and the star man on about his silent business. I close my eyes again.

And hear/feel a creature pad toward my sleeping bag. I feel it touch my right side and curl up next to me. I know it is a bobcat. I am enchanted and yet am afraid to look. I worry that it might be rabid. I wish someone had taught me what to do. I stay inside my sleeping bag, arms tight along my sides, look straight up, and see Orion move.

The cat pads around the top of my head and stops next to my left side. I hear another animal move in. I know that it is a big shrew. I think it is my fear. The bobcat and the shrew begin to fight and I am doubly enchanted, doubly afraid. I scream. . .

. . .and wake myself. My friend mutters something. Orion is gone. I am sad that my fear chased away the cat. I pray to the spirits of the place, tell them we will take nothing and leave nothing. I tell them I am willing to learn what I need to learn. I fall asleep.

In the morning, the sand around my dreaming place is bare. The only tracks are in my heart.

It may be that in dreams, in waking visions,

near rivers, under juniper or willow,

high above our heads or deep in the earth,

cat or otter or crow comes to us

and shows us what we need to see.

It may tell us what we need to know.

It may eat us, it may offer up itself...

*. . .or it may be that we tell ourselves

these dreams and stories, forgetting that, in truth,

we are cat or otter or crow.*

It may be that cat or otter or crow

is far too busy being cat or otter or crow to be

bothered with its two-legged kin.

If we know these things, we might be able to learn something new, we might be able to learn something old and eternal.

Take in your next breath

with all your awareness.

Breathe into your toes,

your fingers, your thighs

and belly and heart.

Breathe into your throat,

your eyes, the places where

your hair springs from your skull.

Breathe into each animal cell

and know that, as you breathe,

so do cat and otter and crow,

so do trout and rattler and hawk,

so do pig and chicken, catfish

and hound, maggot and mosquito. . .

Close your eyes and think

of the great lidless eyes

of salmon, the double lids of owl,

the way the lashes grow thick

over Sophie the Lab's brown eyes...

Imagine yourself on a path

to a place you love.

No human travels with you.

The sky is bright or silvery

or black. Beneath your feet

flows earth or water or air...

. . .you move forward.

Your hear the rhythm

of your animal heart.

You are full of animals,

and animals move outside you,

alongside you, below and above. . .

...one moves close to travel with you.

You hear it before you see it.

You feel the beat of its wings,

know its touch against your leg,

its tongue rough or soft

on your naked hand...

...what is it?

Does it have a name?

Call it by name

and thank it

for joining you.

Ask it to teach you

what you need to learn.

Give it a gift...

. . .go forward. Go back.

Open your heart and listen. . .

...Talasi watched her go.

She was a story, that hawk, more than just

a dark speck against Father Sun...[1]

. . .She was a spirit-hawk

carrying someone's prayers

to the Cloud People;

she was a mother hawk,

carrying rabbit to her baby;

she was a girl hawk,

carrying nothing

but her wild sweet joy,

laughing at Talasi,

so slow and unwinged

on the dusty trail.[1]

What creature has come to you

in your waking moments?

What shadow against the sky?

What eyes bright in woodland darkness?

What flashing on the water,

only the flicker of its passage known?

What creature has come to you

in your times of great joy,

of pain, in your times

of solitude, of kinship.

What creature has come

again and again?

As a girl did you wish

for horses? As a boy,

did you wish the same?

As a child, did you wonder

how the light gleamed a blue

never seen before, off the

raven's back, the butterfly's

wing, the trout's scale?

Was there a special dog?

A kitten? A rabbit or calf or duck?

Once, a friend and I saw

Monarch butterflies swarming

above creekside ferns.

And later, at the base of

a snow-melt cascade,

came across the pure

white skeleton of a sheep,

picked clean, every bone in place.

I took away the jawbone,

a few vertebrae, a legbone

I could not name. A woman

wove the vertebrae into a mask

for me. It still gleams white

and essential in the morning light.

We do honor when we take

away feather or bone or shell.

We do honor when we let them be.

They can be medicine.

They can be memory.

They are always feather or bone

or shell. They are always miracles.

Gliding toward the nest,

a female owl's slow flight

is completely silent.

Its five-foot wing span

makes the great gray owl

the largest in North America.

. . .some owls can hunt

in total darkness.

They locate prey

through triangulation

of sound: dish-shaped facial disks

funnel sounds into their ears,

often from great distances.[2]

Miracles. Tonight,

as you lie waiting for sleep,

imagine what sounds

you wish to hear.

Imagine your spirit's

feathers sprouting.

Imagine you could be

so patient, so silent, so still.

Imagine that in dreams

you fly in total darkness. Imagine

you can hear the light. Listen.

If you are lucky,

if we are both lucky

and wise enough to live

where we have not destroyed

our animal kin, you might

hear coyote's laughter.

You might hear loon's desire.

You might hear wolf's great,

clear, sustained and sustaining

"I am." You might hear

cougar's scream.

Or not. . . "It's just counter to everything the cat stands for, to go around screaming," says Maurice Hornocker, the world's leading authority on cats. "Their whole lifestyle is based on secrecy. . ."[3]

And, it purrs.[3]

If you knew the great that
lived in your heart,
how would it change your life?
Would you be silent?
Would you scream?
Would you keep secrets
that were yours alone?

Would you remember

that there is power

in silence? There is power

in screaming. And, in purring,

perhaps the greatest power of all.

In fact, Belle had purred

right through the dying...

he had purred

clear through the pain,

through the exhaustion

and straight into the release.

He had rarely purred

under human touch.

He just hadn't been that easy.[4]

The kids had come home
one evening with the information
that Belle was a wild cat.
They had seen it on T.V.,
how the Great Cats, the lynx
and pumas and bobcats
did not mew or roar,
"the guy said it," Deej said.
"They sound just like sparrows."[4]

Belle Starr, the dreadful

tom kitten who'd pranced up

to their patio door

with a hummingbird

clenched between his jaws.

He'd opened his mouth

to announce his presence,

and the bird had taken off,

a jeweled streak of right stuff.[4]

Orion and Lepur,

Belle and the ruby-throated bird,

mountain lion and grasshopper,

raven and road-kill, death and me,

death and you. . .those hard dances,

that tricky balance, that clarity. . .

Scotty is very drunk.

He holds Gen's hand in his

as though it were a soap bubble,

trembling, luminous, delicate

as breath. "Up there," he says,

"up near Khe Sanh, the 'Yards

ate the rats, and, later, sometimes

only a little later, the rats

ate the 'Yards. Balance. Clarity." [5]

Though she is afraid,

Gen leaves her hand in his.

"No, Scotty," she says,

"no balance. In between

the 'Yards and the rats,

there was something else.

There was Charlie.

There was us."[5]

We are the only species

to make war on ourselves.

We do not eat what we kill.

We rarely kill what we eat.

And, when we do,

we rarely ask permission.

We rarely give thanks.

Today, tomorrow,

touch your food,

breathe in its smell,

see what it is.

Imagine the horror

of the shipping cars,

the holding pens,

the stench of fear

that fills the air.

Thank the creatures

that became your meal.

Be willing to feel

their terror, know their pain.

What medicine can possibly

come from their deaths?

Pay attention that night

to your dreams.

There is more to this,

more dying, no clarity.

In our national forests,

trees are "harvested,"

mines pierce the earth...

mating and birthing

and nesting places

are torn apart and scattered.

She is mother and sister

to black bear, elk,

wild turkey, antelope,

and big-eared deer.

Above her, in their own

sweet time, soar bald eagle,

red-tail, and turkey vulture.[6]

> When Rex said,
> you're destroying a religious site,
> it means, a robin, when it lays
> its eggs, if you go touch its eggs,
> the mama won't come no more...
> it couldn't be no more.
> There will be no more.
> —Clark Jack, Havasupai tribal leader

No more. When animals come

to us in dreams, when we wear

a silver bear around our neck,

when we believe we know

what power animals can bring,

when we "take" our "elk,"

when we sit in workshops

and take what otter brings us

or fly where raven goes,

do we say thanks?

Sister Raven, Brother Hare,

I owe you so much.

I owe respect.

I owe leaving you alone.

I owe, as an old Earth First!

calendar once said,

more than defense.

I owe vengeance.

Reader, what is your prayer?

Your debt and vow? Your vengeance?

I froze in my tracks,

but too late — he had already

spotted me. This time

he didn't walk away. He ran.

The horselaughing bull [elk] had won

three times running. Fair enough,

I shall pester him no more forever.[8]

Elk are among our best indicators

of wildland's health...[and]

more than mere indicators

of environmental quality.

They are magical beings

that represent all that is magnificent

in nature and wilderness.[8]

. . .signs of their presence

(deep split hoof prints

in the duff, a cast antler,

a bleached thigh bone,

the compressed grass

of a cud bed. . .

that place is forever

transformed in my mind.

That place is sanctified.[8]

Your holy places, those holy signs.

Once, on a Chicago street,

I watched a gang of pigeons

fighting over some french fries.

I saw the light on their feathers,

on silver and green and opal.

They were perfect. The street

was hallowed by their beauty

and their hunger.

Twenty years later, I drive

home from my friend's house.

He lives on the edge

of the Mogollon Rim,

seventy miles from me.

It takes me longer than you

might guess to make the trip.

There are elk. At twilight,

they leap across the road.

Their presence slows me.

A living gift drops

from the Ponderosa.

His head white,

his feathers dappled.

He's young and he plays

with me, flies in front of me,

great talons held close

to his chest.

The young eagle races me,

flying low and powerful.

He swings up over

the top of my truck,

heads straight into the sun.

I lose him. He knows exactly

where I am. Holy. We are.

Once on a dirt road

in the middle of nowhere,

I saw a full school bus stop.

A young sheepdog,

maybe twelve weeks old,

had diverted from its herd

and circled the bus, rounding it up. ⁹

The driver, a Navajo,
and the children understood
and patiently paused
while this useful citizen learned
its trade. . . .Once satisfied
that the bus was under control,
the puppy went back
to bossing the sheep."

The children here grow up

in the belief that they are

one with nature,

no more important

in the scheme of things—

and no less important—

than a piñon pine

or a fresh breeze."

The child in you, the kitten or pup

or bear cub or fledgling, have you taught it

its importance? No more. No less.

Does it know

it is fully animal? Does it honor

that knowledge?

Let it catch a fish and clean it.

Let it leave the fish alone.

Let it climb the stair-step branches

of a young apple tree.

Let it look down.

And see with jay-eyes.

Let it be hungry. Let it eat.

Let it know this:

Before he goes out to hunt,

a Navajo hunter will sing

a prayer to the elk or the deer,

thanking his quarry in advance

for being available to be killed

so the hunter can sustain his life

and that of his family.

The Hopi act similarly.[9]

That's closing the circle — like the hunter's prayer.⁹

Lead the animal child inside

you to the great circle.

The Great Round of elk and wolf

and gutworm and buzzard

and angelfish and ferret

and vireo and goat and all

their relations and yours.

Close the circle. Listen to the singing.

Canis latrans lifts her dark muzzle

against the last Western light.

If she thought words, she would think:

"That is not my name. I am not coyote

or God's Dog or brush wolf.

I know my name. Only I can say it."

And, she does. "Yi-yi-yi-yi-yip-yiiiiiiiiii. . ."

It is [Naturalist Stanley Young said]

as if the coyote let out a prolonged howl,

then ran after it and bit it into small pieces.[10]

And, whale song.

Dark, silver light, bubbles drifting.

We can only guess how that mass

of water presses on their bodies.

We can only guess what ripples

inside them. They sing and sing.

We can only guess that celebration.

Then the approach becomes intense.

On silent feet the cat moves forward,

sometimes putting its hind paws

in the marks made by the front ones

to lessen the chance of a twig snapping

or leaf rustling.[3]

All in the Great Circle know that silence is a song. Be still. Listen to your animal heart, your breath. Sing.

Listen for the song you did not expect to hear.

Cougars also emit birdlike whistles, which are probably used to communicate location and instructions between a female and her kittens.[3]

On your left, a grouse,

on your right, the cowbird.

Astonished, you bow.

Grateful, you let your song

come up from your feet,

the bare feet you have planted

on bare ground.

Cowbird nods. Though he is silent,

you hear a naming song: "Cowbird,"

Vali said. "That's a funny name,"

he said. "I got no regular home;

somebody else raised my kids

and I don't mind; in the right light,

I look good; and I get by."[5]

And your name, your animal name?

Can you remember it? Can you look

into the bright heart of the circle,

into the shadows there and see it?

They had named her Talasi,

pollen, for on her naming day,

the wind had scattered corn pollen

in a golden cloud. For a time,

there had been other names. . .¹

...*Masichuvio,* for the gray deer
seen by her cousin on the morning
of her birth; *Sakapa,* for the pines
climbing Two-Color Mountain;
Muha, for the milkweed's silk.
Those names blew away,
frail as *muha* on the wind.[1]

Deep in the circle's heart,

smoke rises, or cloud or breath

on a mountain morning.

Something takes shape.

It is your name. Vegetable.

Animal. Mineral. An old

and magical game.

Can you guess?

Wapiti? Coyotl? Pesky Varmint?

Catamount? Sea Siren?

*Let it sing
to you. Let it be the music
for your dance.*

The sound is lonely,

eerie, haunting, surreal.

A cry from the deep past.

In a moment there is another.

Then another. Soon the ridges

resound with the chorus

of a wolfpack on the prowl.[10]

Shadows quaver, flow, and become wolves.

Here one, then another, until eight of the beasts

materialize in the moonlight.[10]

The wolf pack exists, of course, to hunt.[10]

Let their song be the music for your hunt.

Let your hunt spin out

from the Great Circle,

from that circle of hunters

and prey, from that circle

of song, that circle of hisssss

and scrrrk and awooooooo.

What do you hunt? What hunts you?

How can you see that dance behind the mirror

of your closed eyes?

For the last ten years of my life

I have danced with raven and crow.

In mourning, I walked under trees

full of crows. I saw the eastern sun set

blood-orange red behind the black branches,

the black birds. That glow, those shadows

illuminated my charred heart.

I've killed very little in my life.

I could not kill the love

that drove me out to walk

at sunset. And so, I came West.

To kill not love, but fear.

To hold a dead raven

in my hands and know

that I had a dance

to make for it.

The wedge-shaped tail, shaggy throat, heavily bristled nostrils, and thick, arched bill are its best field marks. In flight, the raven is magnificent...[11]

. . .alternately flapping and soaring, hovering, diving, and, in courtship, flying wingtip to wingtip and tumble-plunging.[11]

It is mainly a scavenger

and competes with gulls and vultures

for carrion.[11]

The raven lost.

The roadside was bare

except for his dead beauty.

He, she gleamed on the side

of the highway, one wing erect,

pointing to the clear, bright,

desert morning sky.

I drove on to the meeting

where I learn about giving up,

I learn about letting go.

I learn, for the first time

in fifty years, to be fully human,

fully animal, fully woman.

I told my friend I would go pick up

the bird and come back.

He, she was still there.

I bent and touched the wing.

I touched the breast,

the obsidian beak.

He, she was supple,

still warm. I gathered

the raven up.

We stored the raven

in the restaurant freezer

while we held our meeting.

On the next shelf was a tray

of barbequed chicken.

I would think of that later.

The raven rested in my freezer,

while I prayed for the steps to the dance.

I called my friend Dan. On an opal

August night, he came to help me.

He brought his skinning knife.

He brought his sharp knowledge

that I needed to do the work.

The skin peeled away

under the blade.

I broke some bones

and slipped the body

from its feather shroud.

It was no bigger

than a chicken.

Its flesh was dusky

and it smelled fresh.

I rubbed salt into the skin,

hung it by its great wings

in the front porch, in our cool,

dry air. The maggots did

their work, ate out the brain

and a little of the scalp

and skull feathers. "Sid Vicious,"

a friend said, "Trickster."

The raven hangs on my South wall.

Its feet could be carved from black stone.

When I see it, and I cannot look at it

without seeing it, I think of what

I eat. I think of this:

Wherever there is wilderness,

the mellow, drawn-out croak

of the raven is likely to punctuate

the steady whisper of tumbling

water and swaying forests.[11]

I think of my friend

who wrote to tell me

that all he wanted to do

was sit in his cabin

up in the lilac New Mexico light

and listen to the ravens.

Scrkkk. Scrkkk. Scrkkk.

I think of the cats sitting patiently

under the Ponderosa at dawn,

Bad Kitty and Lurch and Moe

and cross-eyed Ray Cooper and Fiona,

and how two ravens buzzed in over them,

quick and bodacious as death.

The cats were still as stone. The ravens laughed and flew away.

And I think of my death

and I am afraid and glad.

I imagine I die near ravens

and I pray to be their food.

To be,

in the Great Circle, fully prey,

then fully predator.

And, perhaps, in the moments

of eating and digestion and cell-becoming,

briefly holy. . .

Every creature, every aspect

of nature has its holy people,

Mike Mitchell, a Navajo medicineman

told me — even the stinkbug.[9]

One does not talk about

such things in nature

when they and their holy people

are present. In winter,

many will have left—bears,

for example—so one can speak

of bears in winter.[9]

For my people, on my mother's side,

nothing ever left and yet we spoke

of everything. On my father's side,

the same. He remembered this:

when the cows lie down, it will rain.

My mother said you could wish

on a white horse. You spit

on your finger, wet your palm

and slap the spot. You don't tell

your wish to anyone...

I can tell you now that I wished

for a horse. Not a white one.

Chestnut, a stallion, then later,

a Welsh pony, fat and furry and slow.

There were legends. A muskelonge as big as a small canoe. He lived beneath the black water of the little lake. Billy Grafton had seen him. His dad had maybe hooked him once and seen the leader snap like thread.

Geese could nip you. Spiders kill.

Snakes wrap 'round your ankle

and poison you in the most

hideous way. And, dogs,

dogs could scare an old lady

(or a little kid) so bad

she'd drop dead from fright.

There were bears in the sky. And rabbits.

Scorpions and goats. You could see them.

You could cover a shoebox with tissue paper,

poke holes in it, put in a flashlight

and have the starry creatures with you

on your bedroom wall or ceiling. . . .always.

My mother's people were Pennsylvania Dutch, my father's, Alsatian. There were stories of werewolves and invisible things that left pawprints, and once, up in the Northern woods, we were sure we heard the howl of the Wendigo, chasing some poor soul who had given in to his fear.

On a summer's day

sometime in the last century,

a frantic Matthew Arbuckle rode

into the community of Papinsville....

He jumped from his horse

and told the gathering crowd

about the terrible monster

he had heard scream...

like the scream of a panther,

only ten times as loud.³

Community leader

Uncle John Whitley

told the assembled men

to gather their hounds

and guns and prepare

to ride out to do battle

with the monster.[3]

Then, around a bend in the river,

came the screaming monster

that had terrified an entire community.

On toward the stouthearted men

it came—a whistle-blowing steamboat

named the "Flora Jones."[3]

Sometimes, the cougar became part of the culture. Aztecs and other Indians attempted to heal their sick with cougar bones, paws, and gall.[3]

"I am Toho," he said, "the old lion."

He held out his thin, twisted hands.

"I do not look like a lion, do I?" he said.

"As you can see, I have no claws."[1]

Monster or magic...in the fine movie
Wolfen, *the Iroquois steelworker says,*
"It's all in the mind." The human mind.

. . .except that my cats chase things

I cannot see. At night, they startle,

stare up at the ceiling, out the window,

toward the black, starry glass

where nothing living seems to move.

My old, cruelly murdered Nessa,

half-husky, half-mistake,

whimpered at the back gate.

And there was nothing there.

I love that I will never know

what moves in their minds,

what leaps in their hearts,

what passes behind the bright

mirrors of their eyes.

The cougar was secretive and mysterious,

and the people feared what they could not see.

Men who had never laid eyes on a cougar

knew in their hearts that if they

ever saw one, they would kill it.[3]

Resume your place

in the Great Circle...

as if you could ever leave...

what creature frightens you,

what creature repels?

There are other teachers.

There are the lessons

you were taught to fear.

Maggots in back-alley trashcans.

I am twenty-three, mother of four,

terrified and wanting very much to die,

wanting very much to not die.

The air is thick and foul. I pour bleach

into the can. The maggots writhe.

There is only silence and the nightmare air.

Twenty-five years later, I watch the maggots eat the raven's eyes. They swarm on its dark skin, speckle its shining feathers. The brain is liquid. It runs like tears from the empty eye sockets. "Thank you," I say.

And later, the raven's skull is clean.

I oil the bill, smooth the feathers

with an old toothbrush. The maggots

are gone. The work is done.

Raven has flown on,

soaring and tumbling

over the mesas to the north,

over the alpine meadows,

where flowers lie thick as stars,

over pewter rivers, over city smoke,

and city and highway, over ocean,

to a brilliant north Atlantic island.

. . .and, nodding to ancestors,

to great Mother Morrigan,

to She who faces Past and Present

and Future all at once, raven flies on,

laughing, over blue ice and temples

and green water. . .

...swings down over northern rain forest, eats salmon, swings down over a red sandstone arch, down, down, to mesa, to ladder, to kiva...

. . .Crow Mother began her descent.

Talasi felt a rush of fear and joy

in her throat. Crow Mother held

a bundle of yucca blades in

Her white arms. Her stern face

was turquoise, Her eyes

white circles, and the place where

Her mouth might have been,

a black triangle. . .[1]

...White eagle down fluttered over Her brow, and shining above Her face rose great raven wings, each feather perfect, each spine a shaft of light. She raised that gleaming head and looked at each child.[1]

The silver rabbit was icy

between Liz's breasts,

the braided silk

the perfect length.

The little charm touched

and swung free, blessing her

with Clara's wishes,

still warm after eight years

and across two thousand miles...[1]

. . .the rock became the tower, and
all—tower, rock, ruined walls—
were eroding back to the glowing
sand. She walked up the road,
her shadow moving ahead of her.
A jackrabbit, its ears translucent
in the dying light, bounded away.[1]

Liz rolled down the window. A big buck jackrabbit leaped straight up a little ahead of the truck. "There he is again," Liz said. "Dime a dozen," Paul said. "No way," she said. "Never. Look at those ears. Look at those moves."[1]

"Oh, spare me," Paul groaned.

"I can't take anymore.

You're gonna tell me

about the relationship

of everything to everything

and Mother Earth

and Holy Rocks. Right?"[1]

If I can tell you that,

how raven is everywhere,

how rabbit is magic,

and maggot and catfish

and seaslug and jay.

If you can tell me

how you are everywhere,

how I am magic,

and neighbor and cousin

and sister and kin. . .

Then, solitude is crucial and tribe a gift...

Each cat respects the other's territorial rights. This technique, called mutual avoidance, probably evolved along with the cougar's solitary life style...[3]

Because it hunts alone

and cannot depend on a pack

for sustenance, the cougar can

ill afford an injury sustained

in defending its territory.

It is to every cougar's advantage

to allow each cougar its private domain.[3]

The wolf's most indispensable personality trait is its ability to exist as part of a group, to form an attachment to others of its kind.[10]

Contrary to popular misconception,

the wolf is generally a docile animal

with a strong aversion to fighting.

Though extremely strong and powerful,

it settles disagreements with others

of its kind through ritualized battle,

not combat.[10]

In a circle of women,

one hunches over herself.

She buries her face in her hands

and cries. Mystic, the Malamute,

pads over, settles herself

with a great sigh and waits

while the woman cries out

the memory of a terrible time,

a terrible touch.

Later, when another in the circle

screams with twenty years

of hidden rage, Mystic moves

quietly to the other room.

As the anger fades away

and the woman begins to breathe

into her peace, the Malamute returns

and settles, with a great sigh,

at the woman's side.

The woman rests her hand
on the dog's big head.
She gives back. We all must:
And I write with the hope
that there will always be
Blue Mountains, always be
a place for the great cats.
Perhaps a little of what I say
will stick, and maybe
somewhere down the road
it will make a difference.[3]

Some species you will probably never see.

Others are familiar to all. And one

or two you may know only as a piercing,

hollow voice in the night. Remember

that sound. And treasure it.[10]

It is old as time,

as wild as the wind,

and as poetic as

moonlight on snow.

It is the trademark

of the wolf and its kin.[10]

Remember. Treasure. Sister Raven. Brother Hare.

Know your place in the Great Circle.

Remember. Treasure. Scrkkk. Yi-yi-yi. Ayiiiii.

Awooooooooooo.

REFERENCES

1.

Mary Sojourner, *Sisters of the Dream,* Northland Publishing, 1989.

2.

Michael S. Quinton, *Ghost of the Forest,* Northland, 1988.

3.

Gary Turbak, *America's Great Cats,* photographs by Alan Carey, Northland, 1986.

4.

Mary Sojourner, "The Late Belle Starr," *Chicago Tribune Literary Supplement,* September 1989.

5.

Mary Sojourner, *Going Through Ghosts* (work in progress).

6.

Mary Sojourner, "There is a Woman," 1987.

7.

Mary Sojourner, "Death of a Mother," *Sedona Tab,* 1988.

8.

David Petersen, *Among the Elk,* photographs by Alan Carey, Northland, 1988.

9.

Suzanne Page, *A Celebration of Being,* Northland, 1989.

10.

Gary Turbak, *Twilight Hunters,* photographs by Alan Carey, Northland, 1987.

11.

Tim Fitzharris, *American Birds,* Northland, 1989.